Spotlight on P...

WHAT KIND OF POEM? 3

Teacher's Book

Contents

Introduction 2

Good Company 4

Two Limericks 5

Dear Spider 6

Ice Dawn 7

Bank Holiday Diary 8

Kenning My Dad 9

From Pen Rhythm 10

Oil Tanka 11

Croc City Rap 12

Cinquain Prayer, February Night, 1349 Cinquain, 1415 Cinquain 13

Elegy for Grandad 14

Sea Lions 15

What am I? 16

The Titanic 17

Huff .18

Write a Poem 19

Dare 20

Photocopiables 21–47

Introduction

Spotlight on Poetry: What Kind of Poem? offers children an experience of the wide range of different forms and styles which poetry can take. This includes, for example, riddles, limericks, sonnets, haiku, cinquains, acrostics, epitaphs, shape poems; poems in the form of alphabets, conversations, diaries, monologues, lists; poems that play with the sounds of words and invent new or nonsense words.

The 20 poems included in *What Kind of Poem?* have been chosen first and foremost because they are powerful and interesting. In terms of both meaning and language, they will catch and hold young children's attention, repaying sustained reading and exploration.

The poems have been chosen also to reflect the range of texts and the objectives in the National Literacy Strategy Framework for Teaching at Key Stage 2. Each poem is related to two terms within Year 5 and Year 6, according to where this match is closest. This means that there is a natural clustering of poems in Year 5 Term 2 and Year 6 Term 2, where different kinds of poems are specified in the objectives and/or in the range of texts identified in the Framework. Detailed notes in this booklet suggest ways in which each poem can be read and explored to develop children's experience, understanding and skill as readers and writers. The substantial and varied activities suggested at Text, Sentence and Word levels provide the basis for a block of integrated literacy work lasting across a week. Working with the poems in this way offers intensive and varied work related to all the poetry objectives, to several other Text-level objectives, and to a large number of Sentence- and Word-level objectives. These objectives are referenced in the notes for each poem.

Spotlight on Poetry materials are arranged to reflect the organisational structures and teaching strategies of the Literacy Hour. Sixteen of the poems are presented in a Big Book anthology for whole class use. All of these plus four additional poems are also presented in a Pupil's Book for group and individual use.

Shared Reading and Writing

Notes on each of the poems in the Big Book describe practical strategies for introducing, reading and exploring the poem in the context of a whole-class interactive session. In doing so, they identify and explain significant and interesting features of the poem. Early activities generally concentrate on developing the children's understanding of and response to the poem's meaning. Later activities focus in on specific aspects of the poem's structure and language at Word and Sentence levels. Of course, many of these, for example, rhyme, rhythm, effects of sound and word choice, recur in different forms in many of the poems; revisiting them in different contexts will help children to consolidate and extend their understanding of poetry. There is also a general movement from reading to writing activities: the content, structure and language of the poem are first explored and discussed, and then used as models for the children's own writing.

Although all of the activities are closely related to the particular poem, some cover more general areas of literacy learning, for example, phonics and spelling, which children will be familiar with from other Word and Sentence level work. Revisiting these areas when exploring a poem sets this learning in context and makes it fun.

Work done in this whole-class context also introduces and prepares the way for independent work later in the Literacy Hour.

You will see that the notes for each poem suggest several different focuses for shared reading and writing. It is the intention that these should be organised across a week of Literacy Hours. The chart shows how this might be planned for *Snowstorm Haiku* and *Electric Haiku* from Big Book and Pupil's Book 2.

Guided Reading and Writing

This section of the Teacher's Notes suggests ways in which you can read and explore the poems in the context of guided group work.

In the case of poems in the Big Book, it is assumed that this phase follows some whole-class work on the poem. The focus here is on close reading and rereading of the text, on extending the children's understanding, and on giving them opportunities to respond in more personal and sustained ways than is generally possible in whole-class sessions. In particular, there are suggestions for developing and supporting writing activities introduced in the shared phase. Again, there are opportunities not only to enrich children's understanding of poetry, but also to develop their experience and skill as readers and writers more generally. The activities have been designed to present varying levels of challenge, and you will need to select ones which are appropriate to the needs of the group with which you are working.

There are also suggestions for reading and comparing related poems within and outside *Spotlight on Poetry: What Kind of Poem?*, for example, poems which are similar in theme, mood or language. You could, if you wish, organise some of this work to give children opportunities to read 'unseen' texts. Well-chosen poems offer ideal material for challenging and developing children's reading strategies and their responses as readers.

In the case of the four poems which appear only in the Pupil's Book, these guided activities will, of course, provide the main focus for your teaching. They follow the same pattern as that for shared reading and writing, beginning with Text-level activities focused on reading, understanding and responding; and moving on to examination of Word- and Sentence-level features of the poem.

Independent Reading and Writing

This section of the notes suggests activities which children can engage in independently, either working together as a group or individually. Most involve developing, extending and applying work introduced in the shared and/or guided phases. There are opportunities in particular for reading and working with related poems and for more sustained writing. In some cases, you may want children to continue this work outside the context of the Literacy Hour. Again, as in guided reading and writing, the activities are at various levels of challenge.

The photocopiable masters included in this booklet provide focused language activities for children to work on independently in this phase of the Literacy Hour.

Planning

Because activities have been focused and devised to fit the structure of the Literacy Hour, work on these poems can be planned flexibly into your overall planning for literacy at termly, weekly and daily levels. Given the wealth of opportunities for literacy learning that the poems offer, we suggest that you use each poem (in the Big Book) as the focus for a week's work. There will, of course, be space within this for you to incorporate activities focused on other aspects of Word- and Sentence-level work.

This chart shows how shared, guided and independent work on *Snowstorm Haiku* and *Electric Haiku* could be planned across a week. The movement is from introducing and exploring the poem at Text level to examining Word- and Sentence-level features; from easier to more challenging work; from reading to writing. The activities for guided work can be repeated, giving you an opportunity to work on the same tasks with different groups. Activities for independent work can be organised in various ways (for example, as a carousel or with all children doing the same activity), depending on how you are structuring tasks in this phase of the Literacy Hour.

Snowstorm Haiku and Electric Haiku

	Shared	Guided	Independent
Monday	● read and discuss *Snowstorm Haiku;* identify conventions for haiku; revise knowledge of syllables and syllable counting	● reread poem, developing understanding and response through discussion; further work on syllables, if required	● count and record syllable patterns in other poems/verses; prepare to present in plenary
Tuesday	● read and discuss *Electric Haiku;* does it follow the rules? ● examine punctuation, and write sentences including similar structures ● use *overheat* as example of compound word; identify others	● read and compare the two haiku ● read and discuss other haiku; compare those in *Spotlight*	● read and discuss other haiku; present favourites as wall posters ● list other compound words
Wednesday	● use *behaviour* and *electricity* as starting point for work on word derivations and related spelling patterns; and/or *kaleidoscope* for work on Greek and Latin word origins	● REPEAT WITH OTHER GROUPS	● PCM: word derivations and spelling patterns ● PCM: Latin and Greek prefixes and suffixes
Thursday	● talk through and demonstrate writing of haiku	● develop writing of haiku, matching support to needs of group(s)	● draft own haiku
Friday	● read drafts of haiku from previous Guided and Independent work; discuss, revise, polish	● help children to revise and polish their own haiku	● revise and polish own haiku; present as wall posters ● plan and prepare performances of their own poems

A final thought

The focus in *Spotlight on Poetry* is on literacy learning: on realising the potential of poetry to extend and enrich children's experience, understanding and skill as readers and writers. It is vital also to give children opportunities simply to enjoy the poems in this collection, and to respond to them personally and emotionally.

Good Company

Leonard Clark

Level   Years 5 and 6
Literacy Focus   Year 5 Term 2 and/or Year 6 Term 3

A sonnet in rhyming couplets, divided into eight and six line sections, each consisting of just one sentence.

Big Book p.3
Pupil's Book p.3

LITERACY OBJECTIVES

WORD

5/2 W3; 6/3 W3 apply knowledge of spelling rules and exceptions
6/3 W6 practise and extend vocabulary
6/3 W7 experiment with language, creating new words

SENTENCE

5/2 S8 construct sentences in different ways
6/3 S4 secure control of complex sentences

TEXT

5/2 T6 understand terms which describe different kinds of poems (sonnet)
6/3 T6 look at connections and contrasts in work of different writers
6/3 T12 compare texts

Shared Reading and Writing

T Read the poem to the children, asking them to follow the text. Prompt them to share first ideas about both its content and its form. Reread the poem with the children, and then examine it more closely. Prompt understanding and response by asking: Who is 'speaking' in this poem? What are the main ideas? Is 'Good Company' a good title? Why? Why not?

W
S Ask the children what they notice about the structure and language of the poem, drawing their attention to:
  ● the pattern of rhyme (in couplets throughout).
  ● the break after line 8, which divides the poem into two parts, each with its own focus.
  ● the structure and punctuation of the two long, complex sentences of which the poem consists.
  ● identify the conjunctions (e.g. *and, when, for, yet, if*) and relative pronouns (*who, that*) which connect clauses.

T During this discussion, explain that poems with 14 lines are called sonnets, and that they can have different patterns of rhyme or be unrhymed.

S Work together to rewrite these two long sentences as a sequence of shorter, simpler sentences.

W Use the words *believe* and *ceiling* to introduce or revise the spelling rule 'i before e except after c'. List words which exemplify this rule, and ones which are the exception to it (e.g. weird, seize).

Guided Reading and Writing

S Reread the poem together, encouraging and helping the children to phrase the long sentences clearly and fluently, using punctuation as a guide.

T Read the poems 'Dear Spider' (Big Book p.5, Pupil's Book p.5) and/or 'Ice Dawn' (Big Book p.6, Pupil's Book p.6) (another sonnet, but with a different pattern of rhyme). Discuss and compare them with 'Good Company', considering content, tone, structure and style.

W Focus on the hyphenated word *soft-scratching*, used in the poem to describe the mouse. Draw out the idea that it is formed by joining an adjective and a verb. Together, write similar words to describe other animals.

Independent Reading and Writing

T Prompt the children to write a report comparing this poem with either 'Dear Spider' or 'Ice Dawn'.

T Suggest the children find and read other sonnets, and to analyse and describe their structures and rhyme patterns.

W Encourage the children to experiment with changing some of the words in this poem, operating at different levels, e.g. changing *chill* to *cold*, or making the mouse the main companion rather than the spider.

Photocopiables 1 and 2: Children look at the letter string *ea* and invent hyphenated words.

Two Limericks

Anon and Traditional

Level   Years 5 and 6
Literacy Focus   Year 5 Term 2 and/or Year 6 Term 2

Two limericks, following the conventional patterns of rhythm and rhyme. The first has the classic opening, in which the place where the subject of the poem comes from is stated.

Big Book p.4
Pupil's Book p.4

LITERACY OBJECTIVES

WORD

5/2 W3; 6/2 W3 apply knowledge of spelling rules; use visual skills

5/2 W5 investigate words with common letter strings but different pronunciations

5/2 W6 distinguish between homophones

SENTENCE

5/2 S1 re-order sentences

TEXT

5/2 T5 perform poems in a variety of ways

5/2 T6 understand terms which describe different kinds of poems (limerick)

5/2 T7 compile anthology with commentaries

5/2 T12 use structure of poems read, substituting words and ideas

6/2 T4 investigate appeal of humorous verse

6/2 T8 analyse success of texts

6/2 T12 study genre and produce piece of similar writing

6/2 T14 write commentaries

Shared Reading and Writing

T Read the first of the two limericks, and ask the children what kind of poem it is and how they know. (This will probably not be the first time they have encountered limericks.) Guide them to identify the characteristic features of this form of humorous poetry, especially the rhythm of lines 1, 4 and 5 and the *aabba* rhyme pattern.

W Read the second limerick. Prompt children to identify similarities and differences between this and the first, noting in particular the use of alliteration and the word play based on homophones *flea/flee* and *flew/flue*. Check that they understand the meaning of the word *flue*.

T Encourage children to discuss why limericks are such a well-known and popular form of poetry. Focus on their brevity, on how the strong pattern of rhythm and rhyme makes them easy to memorise, and on the satisfying surprise or twist usually provided by the last line.

W Use the words *young*, *Gloucester*, *thought* and *sound/found* as the starting point for work on the way in which the same letter string can represent different sound. List other words which follow these patterns. Extend by investigating the sounds of other letter strings, e.g. *ea*, *ow*.

S Discuss the order of words in the second sentence in the first limerick. What is unusual about this? How could the sentence be reordered? For example, 'A sound came from the fridge'.

T Brainstorm and record alternative second lines for each limerick, trying to maintain the rhythm and rhyme.

Guided Reading and Writing

T Continue to find alternative second lines, taking time to revise first attempts to get the rhythm right.

T Read other limericks together. Discuss the extent to which they follow the conventional patterns, and how effective and appealing they are, picking up issues raised in the Shared Reading and Writing session.

W Choose another initial consonant cluster (e.g. *cl*) and see how many different vowel sounds can be added to it to make one-syllable words (e.g. *cl*ue, *cl*ay, *cl*aw). Capitalise on opportunities to revise and extend knowledge of spelling patterns.

Independent Reading and Writing

T Encourage the children to find and read other limericks. They might like to choose a small collection of favourites, and work together to present these to others, either through a live performance with introductions or by compiling an anthology with commentaries.

T Prompt the children to write their own limericks. These could be entirely original, e.g. ones using the name of their home town, or adaptations of ones read, e.g. using the same opening line or couplet.

> **Photocopiables 3 and 4:** Children write limericks of their own and make words from consonant clusters and vowel sounds.

Dear Spider

*Thanks for the invitation
to your cosy dinner for two.
I'd really love to come
but I can't decide what to do.
I can't decide just what to wear
my clothes are all so fine
and I'm not certain where to find
a suitable sort of wine.
I'm not used to dining out,
it's really not my thing.
I tend to snatch meals
when I am on the wing.
My mealtime conversation
is limited in kind
In short I feel that
I really should decline.
It's not that I don't like you
but we are so far apart;
I can't see it working out
although you want my heart.

Yours sincerely
Fly*

Angela Topping

Dear Spider

Angela Topping

Level   Years 5 and 6
Literacy Focus   Year 5 Term 2 and/or Year 6 Term 2

A humorous poem in the form of a letter, organised in five four-line sections in which the second and fourth lines rhyme.

Big Book p.5
Pupil's Book p.5

LITERACY OBJECTIVES

WORD

5/2 W3 build words from awareness of derivations
5/2 W6 distinguish between homophones
5/2 W12 investigate metaphorical expressions and figures of speech
6/2 W5 extend work on word derivations (prefixes, suffixes and roots)

SENTENCE

5/2 S6 be aware of differences between spoken and written language
6/2 S3 revise work on complex sentences (connecting clauses)

TEXT

5/2 T5 perform poems in a variety of ways
5/2 T12 use structure of poems read to write extensions
6/2 T3 recognise how poets manipulate words
6/2 T10 use different genres as models for writing

Shared Reading and Writing

T Show just the title of the poem, and ask children to speculate about its likely form and content.

T Read the poem with the children; groups or individuals could each read a four-line section. Prompt understanding and response by asking: Who is this letter to/from? What is the situation? What are the spider's reasons for turning down the invitation? What is the spider really saying? What story does it remind you of? (Quickly recap the spider's attempts to tempt the fly into its web/parlour).

W Work out and discuss the meaning of *limited in kind*, *in short* and *decline*, and of the idiomatic
S expressions *not my thing* and *can't see it working out*. Brainstorm and record other commonly-used figures of speech.

W Shift the focus to the form and language of the poem, focusing attention on:
S ● the structure and rhyme pattern (see top boxed section above).

   ● the generally informal, conversational tone and language, indicated, for example, by *thanks for the invitation* and *it's not that I don't like you*. Use this as the starting point for identifying and discussing differences between spoken and written language.

   ● the use of logical connectives *but* and *although* to structure the spider's explanation. Identify and discuss these as characteristic of explanatory texts; list other such connectives, and use them in sentences.

W Use the words *two*, *where/wear*, *so* and *wine* as the starting point for work on homophones.

Guided Reading and Writing

T Reread the poem together, paying special attention to intonation and expression.

S Work together to write other explanations for not being able to go to a party, focusing on
T connectives, e.g. I'd like to come but…, I can't come because…, I could come if…

W Use the words *invitation*, *suitable* and *conversation* as the starting point for work on word roots and derivations. Identify the root word in each case; list other words in the same 'family', noting prefixes and suffixes and related spelling rules.

Independent Reading and Writing

S Prompt the children to draw on work from the Shared and Guided Reading and Writing
T sessions to write other excuses, using a range of connectives to write complex sentences.

T Encourage the children to write the invitation that the spider sent to the fly, in the form of a letter poem. Encourage children to follow the structure of this poem or of another form that they are familiar with.

T Suggest the children perform the resulting pairs of poems as dialogues.

Photocopiables 5 and 6: Children write excuses using *but* and write word families for given root words.

Ice Dawn

Patricia Leighton

Level   Years 5 and 6
Literacy Focus   Year 5 Term 2 and/or Year 6 Term 1

A sonnet organised in sections of eight and six lines; alternate lines rhyme, until the last two lines which, unusually, are unrhymed.

Big Book p.6
Pupil's Book p.6

LITERACY OBJECTIVES

WORD

5/2 W3; 6/1 W3 build words from awareness of derivations

6/1 W5 use word roots and suffixes as support for spelling

6/1 W10 use etymological dictionaries to study words of interest

SENTENCES

5/2 S1 reorder sentences

6/1 S1 express sentences in a different order

TEXT

5/2 T6 understand terms used to describe different kinds of poems (sonnet)

5/2 S1 reorder sentences

5/2 T10 discuss effects of imagery in poetry

5/2 T11 use structure of poems read, substituting own ideas

6/1 T3 articulate personal responses to literature

6/1 T5 contribute constructively to discussion of literature

6/1 T10 write own poems, experimenting with active verbs and personification

Shared Reading and Writing

[T] Read, examine and discuss the poem a few lines at a time, as its structure suggests, e.g. the first couplet, the second couplet, the next four lines… Encourage the children to ponder and share ideas about the meaning and impact of these lines, and about the sense of the poem as a whole as it develops.

[W] As this discussion develops, prompt the children to focus on:

[S] ● the meaning of less familiar words, e.g. *strait jacket*, *lethal*, *hoar*, *pulsates*, *opaque*.

[T]   Where appropriate, ask a pair of children to check words in a dictionary while the discussion continues.

● the use of figurative language, both metaphors (e.g. *captured leaves*) and similes (e.g. *like halted thieves*). How does this contribute to the vividness of the description? What ideas and associations does it evoke? Draw out the idea that many natural phenomena in this poem (e.g. the trees, the sun, the garden) are personified – described in terms usually applied only to human beings. Identify words, especially verbs, which create this effect.

● the density of the writing and the sometimes unusual word order, looking especially at how the last two lines/sentences begin.

● the rhyme pattern, distinguishing between full and half rhymes.

● the division of the poem into eight and six line sections. What is the focus of each? Introduce or revisit the term 'sonnet' to describe poems of fourteen lines.

[W] Use the words *granulated*, *pulsates*, *lethal* and *sharpen* as the starting point for work on word roots and derivations. Identify the class of words which generally end with the suffixes *-ate* (verbs), *-al* (adjectives), and *-en* (verbs). List other examples.

Guided Reading and Writing

[T] Read 'Good Company' (Big Book p.3, Pupil's Book p.3), a sonnet with a different rhyme pattern. Identify and discuss similarities and differences between it and this poem.

[W] Explain the purpose of etymological dictionaries; talk through and demonstrate the process of using one to investigate a word which was discussed in the Shared Reading and Writing session (*zip/ped*, *lethal*, *hoar* and *lemon* all have interesting origins).

[W] Brainstorm and record words and phrases that could be used to describe other natural objects,
[T] especially those that can be brought into the classroom, e.g. fruit, vegetables, flowers, etc. Encourage the children to feel, touch, smell and, if appropriate, taste the objects. Prompt them to create similes by likening these objects to other things.

Independent Reading and Writing

[W] Prompt the children to use an etymological dictionary to investigate unfamiliar and/or interesting words which they have encountered recently in their reading.

[T] Suggest the children write a short poem or a passage of descriptive prose which personifies another natural phenomena, e.g. a garden or plant withered in a drought, a rainstorm. Encourage them to focus on verbs which relate the object to the behaviour and action of a human being.

Photocopiables 7 and 8: Children explain the meanings and effect of poetic phrases and write adjectives ending in *al* and *ate*.

Bank Holiday Diary

Friday
We caught the train today at six.
Everyone was packed in so tightly
we felt like a packet of Weetabix.
We were off for a short holiday
at Seaside-over-Sand-in-the-Sticks.

Saturday
The sun shone on our heads all day
making us feel like melted ice cream.
We even felt too hot to play,
lolling around like runny jelly,
wobbling and then dribbling away.

Bank Holiday Diary

Janis Priestly

Level Years 5 and 6
Literacy Focus Year 5 Term 1 and/or Year 6 Term 2

A humorous poem in the form of a diary entry; lines 1, 3 and 5 rhyme in each of the four five-line verses.

Big Book p.8
Pupil's Book p.8

LITERACY OBJECTIVES

WORD

5/1 W10 use adverbs to qualify verbs

SENTENCE

5/1 S1 investigate word order
5/1 S5 understand the difference between direct and reported speech

TEXT

5/1 T7 analyse poetic style (impact of rhymes)
5/1 T17 write metaphors from similes
6/2 T3 recognise how poets manipulate words (rhyme, figurative language)
6/2 T4 investigate humorous verse

Shared Reading and Writing

T Read the poem together; individuals or small groups could take a day each. Prompt understanding and response by asking: Who is the imagined writer of this poem? What is the situation? What happens on each day? How does the 'writer' feel about the events described? Why is there only one word in the diary for Friday? What does this mean and show? Ask the children to retell the story of this holiday, referring to the detail in the text.

T Identify and discuss where the humour of the poem lies, e.g. in the slapstick incident with the packed lunch; in Mum's joke; in the exaggeration; in the final, joyful entry.

Shift the focus to the form and language of the poem, prompting the children to identify and discuss:

S ● the unusual pattern of rhyme. Demonstrate how to record this using letters of the alphabet:
T *abaca*, etc.
   ● the use of direct speech in the third verse.
   ● the use of similes. Identify the first one (*like a packet of Weetabix*), and ask children to find five others. Explain that similes use either the word *like* or *as*. Discuss the impact, especially in creating the humorous effect of the poem.

W Use the word *tightly* as the starting point for work on adverbs. Identify the verb which it
S modifies (*packed*) and its purpose (to add information about 'how'). List adverbs that could be used to modify other verbs in the poem, e.g. shone brightly, roughly threw. Experiment with placing the adverb at different points in a sentence, e.g. Roughly, we threw…; We threw the packed lunch roughly…

Guided Reading and Writing

T Look again at the similes used in the poem. Explain the difference between these and metaphors, and use them as the basis for writing metaphors, e.g. jelly-melting weather, gobstoppers of rain, sardined into the train.

S Examine the punctuation of the direct speech in the third verse. Explain the difference between this and reported speech, and rewrite it in this form, e.g. Mum joked that this was a strange way to keep thin. Transform other examples of direct speech into reported speech, and vice versa.

Independent Reading and Writing

T Prompt the children to read other poems, identifying the rhyme patterns and using letters of the alphabet to record. How many different patterns can they find? They could prepare to present their examples to the class in a plenary session.

T Encourage the children to write other similes to describe the objects, situations and feelings referred to in the poem, e.g. being packed in, feeling hot, being bored.

T Suggest the children write diary entries about a holiday that is a great success. Encourage them to follow the pattern of verse and rhyme in this poem, or another pattern that they are familiar with.

Photocopiables 9 and 10: Children write similes and turn adjectives into adverbs.

Kenning My Dad

Angela Topping

Level Years 5 and 6
Literacy Focus Year 5 Term 1 and/or Year 6 Term 2

A poem based on the listing of kennings: phrases which identify a thing without using its name. There is no regular rhyme, but patterns of sound are created by the repetition of words ending in *-er* and *-ing*.

Big Book p.10
Pupil's Book p.10

LITERACY OBJECTIVES

WORD

5/1 W3; 6/2 W3 apply knowledge of spelling rules
5/1 W8 identify word roots and derivations
6/2 W5 extend work on word derivations

SENTENCE

5/1 S1 investigate word order

TEXT

5/1 T7 analyse poetic style
5/1 T8 investigate examples of word play
6/2 T3 recognise how poets manipulate words (for quality of sound)
6/2 T4 investigate humorous verse (play with meaning)

Shared Reading and Writing

W T Cover up the title and the last three lines. Read the poem together; individual children could take a line each. Invite them to respond to and comment on the poem freely, sharing ideas about both its content and form. Draw out the idea that the poem is clearly about someone but that this someone is not named. Introduce the term 'kenning' to describe phrases which name/identify something without using its name. Find examples of such phrases in the poem, e.g. *a bootstamping coat remover*, *soup inventor*. Who do they think the poem is about? Why? Reveal the hidden text to confirm this and then read the whole poem.

W S Examine the language of the poem in more detail, focusing in particular on:
● patterns of sound, in particular the repetition of words ending in *-er* and *-ing*. There are clear examples in lines 8 and 14.
● the unusual order of words, e.g. *a cheering on at rugby shouter* and *travelling on a train worker*; this is often the result of piling words together to create long phrases which function as adjectives.
● the invention of new words, e.g. *leekbringer*, *bighugging*, by combining two words.

W Focus on the many words ending in *-er* which name someone who performs a particular action, e.g. *praiser*, *remover*, *brainworker*. Identify, in each case, the verb from which these words are derived. Distinguish between real and invented examples, and list others. Note any related spelling rules, e.g. doubling of final consonant in *tapper*. Draw attention to the words *exterminator* and *inventor* which are of the same type but end in *-or*. List other examples, e.g. creator, spectator, conjuror. Explain that there is no rule explaining which words follow which pattern; they have to be learned.

Guided Reading and Writing

T Reread the poem, experimenting with different ways of sharing the text and paying special attention to the phrasing of the complex and unusual language patterns.

W T Choose someone known by everybody in the group; list words ending in *-er* and *-ing* to describe them; encourage the children to try inventing new words through combining shorter words. Look out for opportunities to teach or revise spelling patterns and rules.

W Investigate other ways of forming nouns which describe the performer of an action, focusing in particular on the suffixes *-ian* (electrician, magician), *-eer* (mountaineer, engineer), and *-ist* (scientist, pianist). Note that, unlike nouns ending with *-er*, these are not formed from verbs.

Independent Reading and Writing

W T Divide the group into two. Each sub-group chooses someone known to everybody, and writes a list of words ending in *-er* and *-ing* to describe them. Then the groups should swap and read the other's list, and try to guess who it is.

W T Encourage the children to write kennings to describe objects in the classroom, e.g. a blackboard rubber might be a cloud bringer, an easel might be a straight stander. Ask others to guess what it names.

T Suggest the children write their own poem based on a list of kennings about a friend or family member.

Photocopiables 11 and 12: Children write words describing people and write kennings.

From Pen Rhythm

Benjamin Zephaniah

Level Years 5 and 6
Literacy Focus Year 5 Term 3 and/or Year 6 Term 3

A rhythmic performance poem in two eight-line verses. There is much use of repetition and rhyme, but no regular patterns.

Big Book p.12
Pupil's Book p.12

LITERACY OBJECTIVES

WORD

5/3 W5 investigate and learn spelling rules
5/3 W9 understand how words vary across dialects
6/3 W3 apply knowledge of spelling rules and exceptions

SENTENCE

5/3 S1 secure conventions of standard English

TEXT

5/3 T1 investigate a range of texts from different cultures
5/3 T4 read and rehearse performance poems
5/3 T5 select poetry, justifying choices
6/3 T3 describe and evaluate the style of a poet
6/3 T4 comment on the impact of a poem
6/3 T6 look at connections and contrasts in the work of different writers
6/3 T12 compare texts in writing

Shared Reading and Writing

T Ask children to read the title and to speculate about the subject of the poem: What could 'pen rhythm' mean and refer to?

T Read the first verse together, and reconsider the meaning of 'pen rhythm'. Read the second verse together; prompt the children to develop their understanding of the subject of the poem, looking closely at each line. In particular, prompt children to explore the meanings of the lines *high and low where you can't go* and *the pen plans the rhythm and the rhythm sings the song.* What is the poet saying about writing? About writing poetry?

W Focus on the form and language of the poem, prompting children to discuss:
S ● the personification of the pen and the process of writing, in particular the use of words
T usually associated with human action to create this effect.
  ● the pattern of rhythm and rhyme, noting, for example, the several lines which consist of two balanced parts; the near-rhymes *bubbling* and *cripple it*; the internal rhymes *low* and *go*.
  ● the departures from standard written English (the double negative of *no disease can't cripple*) and the dialect usage of *well strong*. What does this mean? How would they express this idea?

W Use the words *bubbling* and *dancing* as the starting point for revision of spelling rules (dropping of final *e* before addition of suffix beginning with a vowel). Extend by considering addition of other suffixes: *-ed, -able/-ible, -ary*. List other words which follow this pattern. Identify exceptions to this rule, e.g. retaining final *e* in words such as changeable and noticeable to keep consonants *g* and *c* soft.

Guided Reading and Writing

T Reread the poem, and develop the discussion from the Shared Reading and Writing session, giving each child an opportunity to respond more fully. Keep the focus on the style and impact of the poem.

T Read 'Write a Poem' (Pupil's Book p.24). Compare the views of writing given in the two poems. Encourage the children to refer to the text to support and illustrate their ideas.

T If possible read other poems by Benjamin Zephaniah and/or other poets of West Indian origin, e.g. John Agard, Grace Nicholls, James Berry. Identify and discuss contrasts and connections between the work of these writers.

Independent Reading and Writing

T Encourage the children to plan and rehearse a choral performance of this poem. Prompt them to consider pace, intonation and rhythm and ways of sharing the reading within the group.

T Suggest the children continue wider reading of poems by poets of West Indian origin. They could compile a short anthology with a general introduction and commentaries on each poem; or plan a sustained reading aloud presentation of the chosen poems.

T Ask the children to write their own performance poem about doing some other action or process freely and joyfully (e.g. painting or working out a calculation). Or reverse the theme of this poem by writing about what it is like to get stuck on a piece of writing or a sum.

Photocopiable 13: Children add *ing* to verbs.

Oil Tanka

I come from darkness
sucked through giants' drinking straws.
Given refinement,
I burn to air in engines,
die with rainbows in wet streets.

Cedric Sponge

13

Oil Tanka

Cedric Sponge

Level Year 6
Literacy Focus Year 6 Term 1 and/or Year 6 Term 2

A tanka is a Japanese poetry form based on the haiku, but with two additional lines which traditionally acted as a reply to the preceding three lines. The pattern of syllables is 5, 7, 5, 7, 7.

Big Book p.13
Pupil's Book p.13

LITERACY OBJECTIVES

WORD

6/1 W5 use word roots as support for spelling
6/2 W5 extend work on word derivations

SENTENCE

6/1 S2 understand terms active and passive; transform sentences
6/2 S1 investigate further the use of active and passive verbs

TEXT

6/1 T5 contribute to shared discussion of literature
6/1 T10 write own poems experimenting with active verbs and personification
6/2 T3 recognise how poets manipulate words (connotations, layers of meaning)

Shared Reading and Writing

T Conceal the title of the poem: the poem then works as a riddle. Read and reread the poem together. Ask the children: What is the subject of the poem? What does the word *I* refer to? When the children have worked this out, reveal the title. Note the pun *tanka/tanker*, explaining that *tanka* is the term for this kind of poem, which originates in Japan. Reread the poem, considering the meaning and impact of each line in turn. How exactly does this relate to what you know about oil?

W Identify and discuss aspects of the form and language of the poem, focusing on:

T ● the pattern of syllables line by line; remind children of the pattern for haiku, and discuss how tankas extend that form.

● the use of personification, noting that the poem is in the first person and how the choice of verbs brings the inanimate subject to life.

● the use of figurative language and layers of meaning (*giants' drinking straws*, *refinement*, *rainbows*).

W Use the word *refinement* as the starting point for work on word roots and derivations. Identify the root (fine) and list other words derived from it (finest, finery, refinery, finely).

S Focus on the verbs in the poem, distinguishing between those in the active voice (*come*, *burn*, *die*) and those in the passive voice (*sucked*, *given*). Draw out the idea that when verbs are in the passive voice, the performer of the action is not explicitly identified; we do not know who or what gives the oil refinement. Rework this clause in the active voice, e.g. Heat refines me.

Guided Reading and Writing

T Reread and continue discussion of the poem.

W Take other root words (e.g. act, person, appear), and list words that can be derived from them. Capitalise on opportunities for revising and extending knowledge of spelling patterns and rules related to the addition of suffixes.

S Write simple sentences in the active voice, e.g. Becky spilt orange juice all over the floor. Rewrite them in the passive voice (e.g. Orange juice was spilt all over the floor). Note changes in word order and verb form.

T Brainstorm and record ideas for a tanka about some other inanimate object, e.g. a stone, a penny, a chair. Begin to draft and polish these ideas following the form of the tanka, and writing in the first person.

Independent Reading and Writing

T Suggest the children work in pairs to write their own tankas on inanimate objects. If possible, give children the opportunity to use a word processor for this activity, which will involve a good deal of revision.

W Prompt the children to read a page of text from a novel or information book, and to list all the words which are derived from a root word. Ask them to identify the root word, and to list other words which belong to the same 'family'.

T Encourage the children to find and read other examples of poems which depend on the counting of syllables: haiku, tankas and cinquains. You might like to direct the children to the cinquains in this book: 'Cinquain Prayer', '1349 Cinquain' and '1415 Cinquain' (Big Book p.16, Pupil's Book p.18).

Photocopiable 14: Children write a tanka about wood.

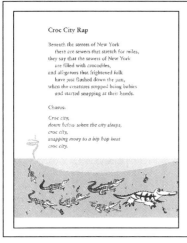

Croc City Rap

Beneath the streets of New York
  there are sewers that stretch for miles,
they say that the sewers of New York
  are filled with crocodiles,
and alligators that frightened folk
  have just flushed down the pan,
when the creatures stopped being babies
  and started snapping at their hands.

Chorus:

Croc city,
down below when the city sleeps,
croc city,
snapping away to a hip hop beat
croc city.

Croc City Rap

Brian Moses

Level   Year 5
Literacy Focus   Year 5 Term 2 and/or Year 5 Term 3

A performance poem in the rap style and rhythm, in three verses with a repeating chorus. (Only the first two verses are printed in the Big Book.)

Big Book p.14
Pupil's Book p.14

LITERACY OBJECTIVES

WORD

5/3 W5 investigate and learn spelling rules

SENTENCE

5/2 S1 re-order sentences
5/2 S5 use punctuation in longer and more complex sentences
5/3 S1 secure conventions of standard English
5/3 S3 identify and use a range of prepositions
5/3 S4 use punctuation marks in complex sentences

TEXT

5/2 T5 perform poems in a variety of ways
5/2 T6 understand terms which describe different kinds of poems (rap)
5/2 T12 use structure of poems read to write extensions, substituting own ideas
5/3 T11 use performance poems as models for own writing
5/3 T4 read and rehearse performance poetry

Shared Reading and Writing

T Focus on the title; ask the children to consider each word in the title and to suggest what the poem might be about and the style in which it might be written. Introduce and explain the term 'rap', emphasising its strong rhythm and quick pace. If possible, play some recordings of rap music to illustrate this.

T Read the first verse and the chorus together. Identify the theme of the poem, and compare it with the children's predictions and expectations. Read the next verse, identifying and discussing how the focus shifts from the general issue to the experience of an individual.

T Reread the two verses and choruses in the Big Book, paying special attention to pace and rhythm. You or a group of children could read the remaining verse and final choruses in the Pupil's Book to complete the poem.

S
T Ask the children what they notice about the form and language of the poem, focusing their attention on:
  ● the structure of the verse and chorus, including how the chorus is doubled and varied at the end of the poem.
  ● the rhyme pattern in the verses.
  ● the structure and punctuation of the complex sentences, especially in the second verse.

S Focus on the first line, identifying *beneath* as a preposition. Reorder this sentence so that the preposition comes at a different point, e.g. There are sewers that stretch for miles beneath...' List other prepositions, and write sentences that start with them.

Guided Reading and Writing

T Read and discuss the whole poem, focusing in particular on the final verse and choruses. What is the focus of this verse? How does it fit in with and continue the preceding verses? Prompt children to work out the meaning of the first line and the name *Dundee* (a reference to Crocodile Dundee).

S Consider the word *ain't*. What is the 'correct' form? Why does the poet use it in this form here?

W Use the words *snapper*, *snapping* and *rapper* to revise work on spelling rules (doubling of final consonant in words ending consonant-vowel-consonant) before inflections and suffixes beginning with a vowel.

Independent Reading and Writing

T Organise the children to plan and rehearse a group performance of the poem. Encourage the children to experiment with pace and rhythm and with different ways of sharing the reading.

T Prompt the children to write a new version of the first four lines of the second verse, substituting a different occupation.

T Suggest the children write a rap poem of their own. A good way into this would be to try substituting a different animal and a different place. Encourage them to plan and rehearse a performance of their poems.

Photocopiables 15 and 16: Children write sentences beginning with prepositions and add suffixes to given words.

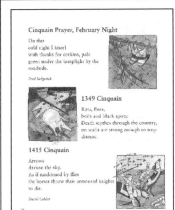

Cinquain Prayer, February Night

On this
cold night I kneel
with thanks for catkins, pale
poem under the lamplight by the
roadside.

Fred Sedgwick

1349 Cinquain

Rats, fleas,
boils and black spots:
Death scythes through the country,
no walls are strong enough to stop
disease.

1415 Cinquain

Arrows
darken the sky.
As if maddened by flies
the horses throw their armoured knights
to die.

David Calder

Cinquain Prayer, February Night, 1349 Cinquain, 1415 Cinquain

Fred Sedgwick and David Calder

Level Year 6
Literacy Focus Year 6 Term 2 and/or Year 6 Term 3

Three varied cinquains, each following the standard pattern with five lines of 2, 4, 6, 8 and 2 syllables. All three are in the Pupils' Book; 'Cinquain Prayer, February Night' and '1415 Cinquain' are also in the Big Book.

Big Book p.16   Pupil's Book p.18

LITERACY OBJECTIVES

WORD

6/2 W3; 6/3 W3 apply knowledge of spelling rules; build words from known words

SENTENCE

6/2 S3 revise work on complex sentences (main clauses, punctuation)

6/3 S4 secure control of complex sentences

TEXT

6/2 T3 recognise how poets manipulate words

6/2 T8 analyse the success of texts

6/2 T10 use different genres as models for writing

6/2 T14 write commentaries

6/3 T4 comment on overall impact of a poem

6/3 T13 write sequence of poems linked by theme and form

Shared Reading and Writing

T Read 'Cinquain Prayer, February Night' to the children, and then reread it together. Give the children time to assimilate and respond to the image that it presents; check that they understand the word *catkins*. Prompt understanding and response by asking: What is the speaker doing and saying in the poem? What is its purpose? (to express thanks, as in a prayer.)

S Focus the children's attention on the form of the poem, challenging them with the question:

T What makes this a poem? Comments on its brevity and density, and its expressive power would be relevant here. Contrast it with narrative prose versions (One cold night I saw some catkins…). Rewrite the text as a prose sentence, and consider how the effect differs.

T Explain that the poem is a cinquain – a form which, like the more familiar haiku, depends on the counting and arrangement of syllables in lines. Ask the children to work out what the 'rules' for this form are.

T Ask the children to read and reread '1415 Cinquain' silently. Does it follow the rules? What is it about? (a battle, specifically the Battle of Agincourt; you could fill in some of the historical background, noting in particular the importance of archers in this battle.) Draw the children's attention to the use of figurative language (the simile *as if maddened by flies*); the line breaks which follow the structure of language and meaning structures more closely than in 'February Night'.

T Discuss and compare the two poems in the Big Book, focusing on their impact and styles.

S Examine and discuss the structure and punctuation of the complex sentence of which 'February Night' consists, beginning *As if maddened…* Identify the main clauses. Note that in the latter example the line break marks the grammatical boundary; in prose, a comma would help the reader here.

W Use the words *darken* and *madden/ed* as the starting point for work on word derivations and related spelling rules (doubling of the final consonant in *mad*).

Guided Reading and Writing

T Reread and develop the discussion of the two cinquains explored in the Shared Reading and Writing session.

S Read and discuss '1349 Cinquain'. What is its subject? (the Black Death.) Does it follow the

T rules? Draw the children's attention to the personification of death as the Grim Reaper; to the poem's arrangement in lines; and to the structure and punctuation of the complex sentence of which it consists.

W Choose a dramatic event from the historical period the children are currently studying.

S Brainstorm and record words, phrases and images which could be used to describe it. Work

T together to draft a sentence which sums up the event vividly. Work this sentence into the form of a cinquain considering word choice, syllable count and line breaks.

Independent Reading and Writing

T Encourage the children to find and read other cinquains. They could choose one, and present it as a wall poster with an explanatory label.

T Suggest the children write a sequence of cinquains about historical events. They could follow the process outlined in the Guided Reading and Writing session.

Photocopiable 17: Children write cinquains about other historical events.

Elegy For Grandad

There's a photo of my Grandad
On the wall in the hall.
He's a tiny man with a white moustache.
In his wrinkled hand there's a thin cigarette
Which is dripping grey, sinister ash.

I was five, I think, when we first met.
It was the last time too.
And yet
I have to say
I remember him clearly still today.
More than sixty long, long years away.

The memory of how he kindly played with me,
Although he was then so slowly dying,
Has firmly stayed with me.
He was the gentlest of men.
I fear I shall not see his like again.

John Kitching

Elegy for Grandad

John Kitching

Level Years 5 and 6
Literacy Focus Year 5 Term 2 and/or Year 6 Term 2

An elegy in three five-line stanzas in which there is some use of rhyme but no regular pattern. The poem is conversational in style and tone.

Big Book p.17
Pupil's Book p.19

LITERACY OBJECTIVES

WORD

6/2 W5 extend work on word origins, using range of dictionaries

SENTENCE

5/2 S5 use punctuation to signpost meaning in more complex sentences

6/2 S3 revise work on complex sentences (main clause, use of punctuation)

TEXT

5/2 T5 perform poems in a variety of ways

5/2 T6 understand terms which describe different kinds of poems (elegy)

5/2 T12 use structure of poems read, substituting own ideas

6/2 T3 recognise how poets manipulate words

6/2 T5 analyse how moods and feelings are conveyed in poetry

6/2 T12 study a genre and produce similar piece of writing

Shared Reading and Writing

W T Read the poem to the children, encouraging them to respond to it freely. Reread the poem together, prompting understanding and response by asking: Who is speaking in the poem? How old is this speaker? (we can deduce that he/she is about 65 years old.) Why is the ash described as *sinister*? What is the meaning and effect of the final line? What is the tone and mood of the poem? (serious, thoughtful.) What do you think an 'elegy' is? Introduce and define this term.

W T Switch focus to the form and language of the poem, prompting children to identify and discuss:
- the patterning of the verses, noting where and how rhyme is used but that there is no regular scheme.
- the vivid descriptive detail achieved, especially in the first verse, through the use of adjectives (*tiny, white, wrinkled, thin, grey, sinister*) and adverbs (*clearly, kindly, slowly, firmly*). If appropriate, take the opportunity to revise the function and form of these word classes.
- the conversational style of the poem, especially the second verse (indicated by the phrases *I think* and *I have to say*).

W Use the word *sinister* as the starting point for investigation of word origins and the purpose and use of etymological dictionaries. The original meaning relates to left-handedness.

S Examine the structure and punctuation of the complex sentences beginning *In his wrinkled hand...* and *The memory of how...* Identify main and subordinate clauses.

Guided Reading and Writing

T Read and discuss other elegies, noting differences in tone and style.

S Write complex sentences modelled on the structure of the two identified above. With the latter example, draw attention to the use of punctuation to demarcate the embedded subordinate clause.

W Choose a text with challenging and unusual vocabulary. Ask the children to read this; to identify and discuss interesting and unfamiliar words; and to use dictionaries to investigate their meaning, derivations and origin.

Independent Reading and Writing

T Prompt the children to plan and rehearse a performance of this poem (or another elegy) which brings out its tone and style.

T Suggest the children choose a person or thing that they miss and remember fondly; the person need not be someone who has died, but could instead be a friend who has moved away. Ask them to write their own elegy, in prose or poetry. Encourage the children to use vividly descriptive language.

Photocopiables 18 and 19: Children write vivid descriptions of someone they know and use an etymological dictionary to find definitions.

Sea Lions

Valerie Worth

Level   Year 5
Literacy Focus   Year 5 Term 1 and/or Year 5 Term 2

This descriptive poem in 19 short lines uses the sounds of words to reinforce the meaning.

Big Book p.18
Pupil's Book p.20

LITERACY OBJECTIVES

WORD

5/1 W7 explain differences between synonyms; identify shades of meaning
5/2 W4 explore spelling patterns of consonants and formulate rules
5/2 W11 explore onomatopoeia

SENTENCE

5/1 S6 understand use of punctuation as an aid to the reader

TEXT

5/1 T6 identify what is distinctive about style of a poem
5/1 T7 analyse and compare poetic styles
5/1 T8 investigate word play, relating form to meaning
5/1 T17 write metaphors
5/2 T5 perform poems in a variety of ways
5/2 T10 understand differences between literal and figurative language
5/2 T12 use structure of poems read, substituting own words and ideas

Shared Reading and Writing

W
T Encourage children to share what they know about sea lions, focusing on their appearance and behaviour. List words and phrases which could be used to describe them.

W
T Read and reread the poem. Prompt the children to share lines, words and images that they find especially memorable and effective. Relate the poem to the earlier discussion of sea lions: How precisely and effectively does the poet succeed in describing them?

T Switch focus to the form and language of the poem, prompting the children to identify and discuss:
- how it is organised in lines, and the effect this has on the reader – particularly clear at the break *climb/Up*.
- how metaphor (*satin sea lions*) and simile (*like soft boulders*) contribute to the vividness of the description.

W
S
T - the choice of words, chosen not just for their meaning but also because of their sounds. Note how this evokes and mirrors what is being described (e.g. *satin sea lions*, *sink down*, *slide/In swift circles*) and the use of onomatopoeic words in *slapping/Their flippers*. Prompt the children to consider possible alternatives and how the meaning and effect would differ if the alternatives had been used instead.
- how the approach shifts in the last four lines from description to general comment and conclusion, and how this is introduced and signalled by a colon.

W Use the words *circle* and *cement* as the starting point for work on 'soft' *c*, and the words *flipper* and *slapping* to exemplify the rule for doubling final consonants.

Guided Reading and Writing

T Reread the poem and work together to get the phrasing and intonation just right – a challenging task.

T Read other descriptive poems about animals. Discuss and compare them with this poem, noting similarities and differences, and focusing on style and structure.

W
T Choose another animal. Brainstorm and record words and images that could be used to describe its appearance, movement and behaviour. Prompt children to consider the precision of their word choices, and how the sounds of words could contribute to the power of the description. Begin to draw on this word bank to write a poem about the animal.

Independent Reading and Writing

T Prompt the children to plan and rehearse a performance of the poem for an audience, paying special attention to phrasing and expression.

T Encourage the children to read other descriptive poems about animals. They could choose a favourite, and prepare to introduce and present it to the rest of the class in a plenary session.

T Suggest the children write their own descriptive animal poem using 'Sea Lions' as a model and drawing on work from the Guided Reading and Writing session. Prompt the children to follow the detailed description with lines which make a general comment and bring the poem to a conclusion.

Photocopiables 20 and 21: Children write synonyms and definitions for words from the poem and write a poem of their own.

What am I?

Judith Nicholls

Level Year 6
Literacy Focus Year 6 Term 2 and/or Year 6 Term 3

A riddle written in the first person, in two four-line verses in which the second and fourth lines rhyme. (The answer is candyfloss.)

Big Book p.22
Pupil's Book p.27

LITERACY OBJECTIVES

WORD

6/2 W2; 6/3 W2 use known spellings as basis for spelling other words

6/3 W6 extend vocabulary through inventing word games (riddles)

6/3 W7 experiment with language (new words, similes, metaphors)

SENTENCE

6/2 S3 revise work on complex sentences (use of punctuation)

6/3 S4 secure control of complex sentences

TEXT

6/2 T3 recognise how poets manipulate words (figurative language)

6/2 T4 investigate humorous verse (play with meanings)

6/2 T10 use different genres as models for own writing

6/3 T13 write a sequence of poems linked by theme or form

Shared Reading and Writing

T Conceal the second verse of the riddle. Read the first verse together, and ask the children if they know what the answer is. Reveal and read the second verse to gather more clues and/or to confirm or refute any answers already offered.

T Discuss the form and language of the riddle, focusing on:
- the pattern of line and verse.
- the use of personification (the riddle is written as if the subject, the candyfloss, were speaking).
- the use of figurative language, prompting children to identify the metaphor (*a puff of pink smoke*) and the simile (*like a small duvet*). Note how this contributes both to the vividness and the fun of the poem.

W Focus on the invented hyphenated words *chin-sticker* and *lip-gripper*. Discuss how these are
T formed (noun naming part of body plus noun derived from a verb and describing the performer of an action). Using ideas from the second verse, invent other words like this (finger-clinger, thumb-curler, tongue-wrapper). Extend to inventing words to describe the effect of other kinds of food, e.g. ice lollipops, crisps, chocolate.

S Identify and discuss the structure and punctuation of the single sentence of which each verse
T consists, noting in particular the use of semi-colons. In the first verse this creates a stronger break than would a comma; in the second it links the two parts where a full stop would separate them. Rewrite each verse, dividing it into two sentences. (In the first, words will need to be added, e.g. I am a chin-sticker…) Discuss how the effect differs.

Guided Reading and Writing

W Use the words *thumb*, *duvet*, *wrap* and *tongue* to revise work on less common spelling patterns. Note what is unusual about these words; find others which follow the same patterns. Give the children a challenging text, and ask them to identify other unusual patterns.

T Read other sophisticated riddles (examples can be found in collections of nursery and traditional rhymes) and work out the answers. Discuss the variety of forms and tones which this kind of poem can take, e.g. humorous, serious.

W Choose another kind of food or drink. Brainstorm and record similes and metaphors to
T describe what it is like; and hyphenated words like *chin-sticker* to describe what it does. Draw on this to write a riddle.

Independent Reading and Writing

T Encourage the children to find and read other riddles. They could choose favourites and then find a way of presenting them to others so that the answer is concealed during reading but available afterwards.

T Suggest the children write their own food and drink riddles, following the pattern and style of this poem or another which they have read. The group could work together to produce a sequence of poems, e.g. School Dinner Riddles.

W Prompt the children to compile lists of words illustrating unfamiliar spelling patterns. This could then be designed as a wall poster for others to use as a spelling resource.

Photocopiable 22: Children invent descriptive hyphenated words.

The Titanic

Andrea Lewis

Level Years 5 and 6
Literacy Focus Year 5 Term 1 and/or Year 6 Term 3

A descriptive poem in four unrhymed verses of five lines each. The sounds of words are used to create the mood and make the scene more vivid.

Big Book p.20
Pupil's Book p.28

LITERACY OBJECTIVES

WORD

5/1 W3; 6/3 W3 build spellings using suffixes; apply knowledge of spelling rules

5/1 W7 explain differences between synonyms

5/1 W8 identify word roots, derivations and spelling patterns

6/3 W5 invent words using known roots and suffixes

6/3 W7 experiment with language (creating new words)

SENTENCE

5/1 S6 understand the need for punctuation

5/1 S8 revise and extend work on verbs

TEXT

5/1 T7 analyse and compare poetic styles

5/1 T16 convey feelings and moods through careful choice of words

5/1 T17 write metaphors

6/3 T3 describe and evaluate style of individual poet

6/3 T4 comment on impact of poem

6/3 T7 annotate text in response to questions

Shared Reading and Writing

T Encourage children to discuss what they know about the Titanic, and in particular to imagine what it would look like lying wrecked on the sea bed.

T Read the poem with the children. Prompt them to share first impressions, considering content, mood and style. Reread the poem, identifying the focus of each verse, and discussing its meaning in detail.

W Prompt the children to develop their discussion of the form and style of the poem, asking:
S What do you notice about the way this poem is written? Prompt them to focus on:
T ● the organisation of the poem in verses, noting that there are no regular patterns of rhythm or rhyme.
● the power and precision of the words chosen, e.g. *raging, spilled, stilled, murky, lurk, massive*. Consider alternative choices, and shades of meaning.
● how the sounds of words are used to evoke the scene and the mood more vividly, e.g. in the phrases *dark green gloom, shifting shape of the ocean sand/softly sighing*; note also the frequent use of *s* and *sh* sounds in the second and third verses.
● the use of figurative language in the metaphorical use of *guts* and in the similes *as if crushed by a giant's fist* and *like eyelashes with tears*.

W Use the words *wildest, raging, watery, dangling, bubbling* as the starting point for revision of word derivations, suffixes and related spelling rules.

S Discuss the use of verbs in the poem, e.g. identify the main verbs in each verse/sentence (*lie* in first verse); use of the passive voice in the second verse (*is stilled*); use of the present tense.

Guided Reading and Writing

W Reread the poem together. The dense style and wide vocabulary make this a
T challenging a text.

S Draw children's attention to the fact that the poem is unpunctuated. Ask them to imagine it as prose: What punctuation marks could be added to help the reader? For example, in the second verse, commas could be added after *swells* and *slime*; a comma, semi-colon or dash added after *stilled*.

W Focus on the invented or at least very obscure word *rusticle*. What is the root word? What is the suffix? What does it mean? (The suffix *-cle* suggests a small part of something.)

Independent Reading and Writing

W Prompt the children to use a dictionary of synonyms to identify and define words that are similar in meaning to ones used in the poem (and discussed in the Shared Reading and Writing session).

W Invent other words ending with the suffix *-cle*, e.g. the last inch or so of a pencil might be a pencicle. Invent new words ending with other suffixes, e.g. *-hood, -ish, -ship, -age*.

W Suggest the children write another verse for this poem, e.g. about a particular part of the ship
T or finding a skeleton. Encourage them to pay special attention to word choice, considering both meaning and sound; to experiment with metaphors and similes; and to maintain the mood of the original poem.

> **Photocopiables 23 and 24:** Children underline interesting and important words from the poem and explain why the poet might have chosen these words. (Note: this photocopiable continues over two pages.)

Huff

I am in a tremendous huff –
Really, really bad.
It isn't any ordinary huff –
It's one of the best I've had.

I plan to keep it up for a month
Or maybe for a year
And you needn't think you can make me smile
Or talk to you. No fear.

I can do without you and her and them –
Too late to make amends.
I'll think deep thoughts on my own for a while,
Then find some better friends.

And they'll be wise and kind and good
And bright enough to see
That they should behave with proper respect
Towards somebody like me.

22

Huff

Wendy Cope

Level   Years 5 and 6
Literacy Focus   Year 5 Term 2 and/or Year 6 Term 2

A witty, ironical poem in six four-line verses in which the second and third lines rhyme.

Pupil's Book p.22

LITERACY OBJECTIVES

WORD

5/2 W12 investigate metaphorical expressions and figures of speech

SENTENCE

5/2 S4 revise function of pronouns
5/2 S6 be aware of use of punctuation to replace pauses
5/2 S10 ensure that pronoun reference is clear

TEXT

5/2 T12 use structure of poems read, substituting own ideas
6/2 T4 investigate humorous verse
6/2 T5 analyse how feelings and attitudes are conveyed in poetry
6/2 T6 read and interpret poems in which meanings are implied

Guided Reading and Writing

W Discuss the meaning of the word *huff* of the title. Read the poem right through together,
T e.g. sharing verses round the group. Share first thoughts and responses.

W Reread the poem, pausing after each verse to identify and discuss the development of the
T 'speaker's' thoughts and feelings. Check that the children understand the words *amends* and *heady*. In particular, prompt them to discuss what is implied by the final verse (maybe the huff is not going to last as long as planned in the second verse!) and whether they think the poem is humorous or serious. This discussion should help children to appreciate the poet's use of exaggeration and irony to convey the speaker's self-regard and self-delusion.

W Examine the form and language of the poem, noting in particular:
S ● the patterns of verse and rhyme.
   ● the conversational style and tone, indicated by phrases such as *really, really* and *no fear* and by the use of dashes in loosely constructed sentences.

W Use the expressions *keep it up*, *deep thoughts* and *cold fury* as the starting point for investigating commonly-used metaphorical expressions. Collect and discuss the meaning of similar expressions.

S Identify the pronouns used in the poem, and the person, persons or things to whom they refer.

Independent Reading and Writing

T Prompt the children to plan and rehearse a performance of this poem which brings out the feelings of the speaker and the humorous tone.

W Suggest the children collect other metaphorical expressions. These could be presented as a wall display or poster and added to continually.

T Ask the children to write about other emotional situations, either in prose or using an appropriate poetry form that they are familiar with.

Photocopiable 25: Children write a monologue from the point of view of one of the friends mentioned in the poem.

Write a Poem

Olive Dove

Level　　　　　　Years 5 and 6
Literacy Focus　Year 5 Term 1 and/or Year 6 Term 2

A monologue in free verse, but with some elements of patterning.

Pupil's Book p.24

LITERACY OBJECTIVES

WORD

5/1 T7 explain differences between synonyms

SENTENCE

5/1 S5 understand the difference between direct and reported speech

TEXT

5/1 T8 investigate and collect examples of word play

6/2 T3 recognise how poets manipulate words

6/2 T6 read and interpret poems in which meanings are implied

6/2 T8 analyse success of a text

6/2 T14 write commentaries

Guided Reading and Writing

[T] Read the poem together, perhaps taking a section each. Discuss the situation; the speaker of the poem and her/his response to it; the response of the other children. Guide children to identify and appreciate the irony at the heart of the poem: the writer has made a poem about not being able to write a poem; in saying that she/he has nothing to say, the writer finds something to say and says it powerfully. A good way of raising this issue would be to draw attention to the final line, and ask did he/she really have nothing to say? In relation to this, note how the style becomes more vivid and 'poetic' in the two long sections beginning *I thought of fighting cats* as the writer gets into her/his stride and finds something to say.

[W] Discuss the form and language of the poem, focusing on:
[T] ● its organisation in lines, and how this reflects and reinforces the flow of thought, e.g. in the two single-line sections, and in the section beginning *Stephen straightaway...* Consider how the effect would differ if the text were set out as prose.
● elements of patterning, e.g. in the first four lines of the penultimate section.
● word choice. Discuss the vividness of, for example, *snatched*, *tossed*, *strewn*, considering their precise meaning and distinguishing them from close synonyms. Identify and discuss the unusual onomatopoeic words *fuzzing* and *tittering*, which introduce an element of word play into the description.

[S] Use the first section of the poem to revise knowledge of the punctuation and setting out of direct speech. Rework this as reported speech, e.g. Our teacher told us to write a poem. She said that it could be about anything...

Independent Reading and Writing

[T] Encourage the children to read other monologue poems. Examples in this Spotlight collection include 'Good Company', 'Elegy for Grandad' and 'Huff'. Identify and discuss similarities and differences in style and form. Children could contribute a favourite poem to a short anthology, and write commentaries explaining why they think it is successful.

[W] Prompt the children to find or invent vivid and/or onomatopoeic words to describe the sound of other activities.

[T] Suggest the children write a monologue poem about being asked to do something in school which they do not want to do or feel they are unable to do. Prompt them to use features of 'Write a Poem', e.g. beginning with speech, including the responses of other children, and to pay special attention to conveying the intended feeling, e.g. desperation, frustration, boredom.

Photocopiable 26: Children use real or invented words to describe sounds.

Dare

Margaret Blount

Level Years 5 and 6
Literacy Focus Year 5 Term 1 and/or Year 6 Term 2

A conversation poem using direct speech.

Pupil's Book p.30

LITERACY OBJECTIVES

WORD

5/1 W9 collect and classify idiomatic phrases

SENTENCE

5/1 S5 understand the difference between direct and reported speech
5/1 S7 understand how dialogue is set out

TEXT

5/1 T7 analyse and compare poetic styles
6/2 T3 recognise how poets manipulate words
6/2 T10 use different genres as models for writing

Guided Reading and Writing

T Choose two children to read the poem, alternating lines/parts. Repeat with a different pair. Discuss what is going on in the poem. Draw children's attention to the fact that the subject of the dare and the identity of those involved in the argument are never stated. Encourage speculation about what and who this might be. Ask children to identify and explain the point that the poem makes about bravery.

S Use the text to reinforce understanding of direct speech: the poem consists of the words that the 'characters' actually spoke – and nothing else. Ask children to identify what is unusual about the way the dialogue is presented: 'sentences' of speech do not end with full stops. Show where these would go (inside the closing speech marks). Explain the use of single speech marks within double speech in the last line.

S Rework the poem as reported speech; to do this you will need to name, or in some way identify, the speakers, e.g. Molly told Sally that she was chicken. Sally replied that she was not. Draw the children's attention to what needs to be changed and added.

W Use the expression *You're chicken* as the starting point for work on idioms. A good focus for this would be to collect others involving animals, e.g. catty behaviour, dogging someone's footsteps.

Independent Reading and Writing

T Encourage the children to read and discuss other conversation poems, comparing them with this one (e.g. 'Rodge Said', *What Kind of Poem? 2*, Big Book p. 18, Pupil's Book p.22). They could choose a favourite and plan and rehearse a performance.

W Suggest the children collect more idioms. Design, write and illustrate a wall poster to share them with others.

S Ask the children to write a conversation poem using direct speech only about some other
T argument. Prompt them to find a way of bringing it to a firm and satisfying conclusion.

Photocopiable 27: Children write down animal idioms.

The letter string **ea** can be pronounced in different ways.

as in fl**ea**   as in thr**ea**d

Write the words for these things in the correct column.

Then add more words of your own.

ea as in fl**ea**   **ea** as in thr**ea**d

_____   _____

_____   _____

_____   _____

_____   _____

_____   _____

_____   _____

_____   _____

Good Company

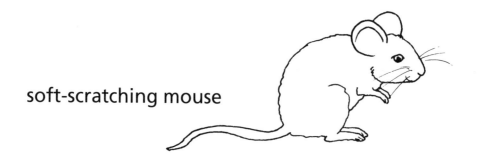

soft-scratching mouse

Write **hyphenated** words to describe the things below.
You can use **adjective + verbs**, as in the example above.
Or **noun + verb** as in 'cat-dodging'.

snail	cobweb
wasp	butterfly

Choose and draw two things of your own choice.
Write hyphenated words to describe them.

Write the second line for limericks which start like this:

There was a young lady from Devon

There was a young person from Ealing

There was an old lady from Lancing

There was a young lady from Gower

There was a young person from Purley

There was an old lady from Settle

There was a young lady from Harrow

There was a young person from Eton

There was a young person from Hitchin

Which beginnings give you ideas for
the next three lines?
Choose some and write complete
limericks.

Two Limericks

| flea fly flew flaw |

Add **vowel** sounds to these initial **consonant** clusters to make three one-syllable words.

cl _____   _____   _____

pl _____   _____   _____

sl _____   _____   _____

cr _____   _____   _____

tr _____   _____   _____

gl _____   _____   _____

Choose two sets of words.
Write a sentence for each set which includes all three words.

_____

_____

_____

_____

_____

_____

Collins *Spotlight on Poetry* Activity Masters
© HarperCollins*Publishers* 1999

I'd really love to come
***but** I can't think what to do.*

It's not that I don't like you
***but** we are so far apart;*

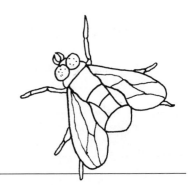

Use the conjunction **but** to write
excuses explaining why you...

haven't done your homework

are late for school

can't do PE today

can't go to a party

forgot to deliver a message

Make up excuses for other things.

Several words can be derived from these root words from the poem.

Write a word family for each of them.

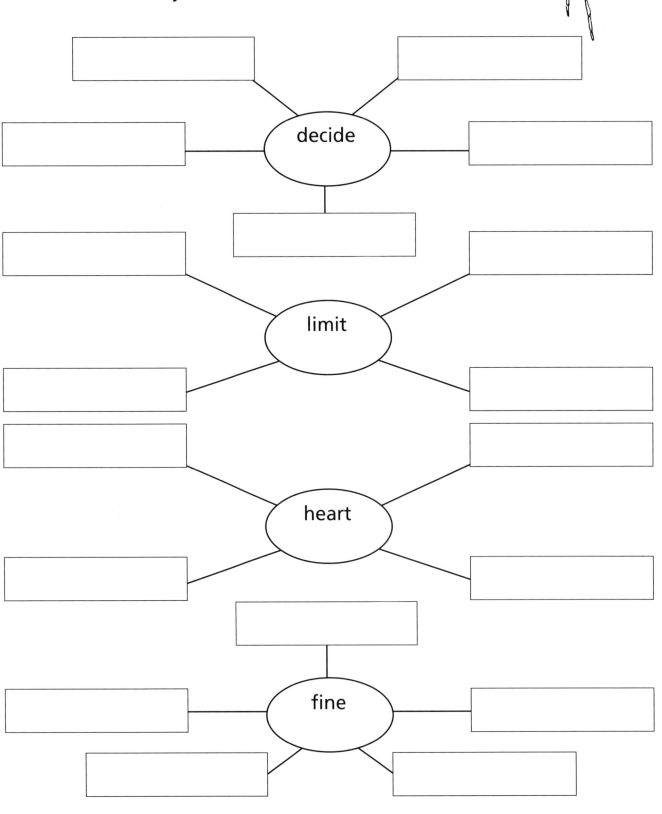

Collins *Spotlight on Poetry* Activity Masters
© HarperCollins*Publishers* 1999

Ice Dawn

Write explanations of the meaning and effect of these words and phrases from the poem.

helpless arms of tall trees
lethal needles
captured leaves
a lemon sun pulsates
dawn's tight fist

Write down another word or phrase from the poem that you find interesting and powerful.

Explain its meaning and effect.

Ice Dawn

lethal needles

The letter string **al** is a common ending for **adjectives**.

Write down the adjectives ending in **al** that are derived from these root words.

Then add other words to the list.

use _____   music _____

nature _____   origin _____

type _____   practice _____

person _____   digit _____

centre _____   accident _____

The letter string **ate** is a common ending for verbs.

puls**ate**   granul**ate**   refriger**ate**

Write a list of verbs ending in **ate**.

Collins *Spotlight on Poetry* Activity Masters
© HarperCollins*Publishers* 1999

Bank Holiday Diary

In this poem, the poet uses **similes** to describe feelings and situations vividly.

> bored as planks on a pirate ship
> packed like canned sardines

Choose a school routine.

assembly	playtime	lining up	dinner-time
	wet play	taking the register	

Write down words that describe this routine and how you feel about it.

_____ _____ _____

_____ _____ _____

_____ _____ _____

_____ _____ _____

Use some of your words to write similes to describe the routine more vividly.

Use these similes to help you write a poem.

packed tightly

The word **tightly** is an **adverb** derived from the adjective **tight**.

Remember: you can't always just add ly.

Turn these adjectives into adverbs.

slow _____   tidy _____

real _____   noisy _____

awful _____   sensible _____

giggle _____   busy _____

happy _____   useful _____

wrinkle _____   horrible _____

easy _____   normal _____

steady _____   greedy _____

sudden _____   quiet _____

hungry _____   comfortable _____

lazy _____   lucky _____

freckle _____   careful _____

simple _____   angry _____

Write two spelling rules for the formation of adverbs ending in **ly**.

1. _____

2. _____

Collins *Spotlight on Poetry* Activity Masters
© HarperCollins*Publishers* 1999

Kenning My Dad

If you watch birds, you are a birdwatch**er**.
If you invent things, you are an invent**or**.

Words for a person who performs a particular action are often formed by adding the suffix **er** or the suffix **or** to the verb.

List more words that end in these suffixes.

-er	-or

Words for people who do particular things can also end with the suffixes **ist**, **eer** and **ian**.

pian**ist**   engin**eer**   music**ian**

List more words ending with these suffixes.

-ist	-eer	-ian

Collins *Spotlight on Poetry* Activity Masters
© HarperCollins*Publishers* 1999

pudding praiser   bighugging   loudlaughing   funloving

Choose someone you know very well –
a friend or a member of your family.

Make up words ending in **ing** and **er** to
describe them and what they do.

-ing	-er

Use these words to help you write a list of kennings about
this person.

Kenning for _____

Collins *Spotlight on Poetry* Activity Masters
© HarperCollins*Publishers* 1999

Add the ending **ing** to these verbs.

Remember: sometimes you cannot just add this ending. You will have to change the spelling of the root word first.

bubble _____

shake _____

prod _____

forget _____

dance _____

dash _____

cheat _____

agree _____

carry _____

bury _____

rage _____

hope _____

jog _____

tug _____

grin _____

help _____

whip _____

compare _____

boil _____

close _____

end _____

dust _____

trot _____

begin _____

moan _____

scribble _____

scrap _____

skip _____

decide _____

scrub _____

Write the spelling rules.

1. _____

2. _____

Oil Tanka

Think about wood.

List words and phrases that you could use to describe…

what it looks and feels like   where and how it grows
how it is used   what it is used for

_____   _____   _____

_____   _____   _____

_____   _____   _____

_____   _____   _____

_____   _____   _____

Use these words and phrases to help you write one or two sentences about wood.

Rework the sentence or sentences into the form of a tanka.
You can add words, take away words, change words.
Carry on rewriting until it is just right and follows the pattern of syllables exactly.

Collins *Spotlight on Poetry* Activity Masters
© HarperCollins*Publishers* 1999

Beneath the streets of New York
down below when the city sleeps

These sentences from the poem begin with **prepositions**.

Choose a subject with lots of movement to write about.

| a dog in the park? a cat chasing a mouse? playtime? |

Write sentences about it beginning with these prepositions.

| Into |
| Under |
| Through |
| Across |
| Behind |
| Between |
| Along |

Rework and redraft your sentences to make a poem.

Collins *Spotlight on Poetry* Activity Masters
© HarperCollins*Publishers* 1999

Croc City Rap

stopped   snapping   rapper

These words from the poem are formed by adding the suffixes **ed**, **ing** and **er** to the root words **stop**, **snap** and **rap**.

The final consonant is doubled before these suffixes are added.

Add the suffix **ed**, **ing** and **er** to these root words. Write the new words down in the correct column. Then add more words of your own to each list.

pop ask play begin grin stretch frighten chat beg
help add scrap kidnap start polish sprint cram

just add suffix	double final consonant before adding suffix

Explain the rule for adding these suffixes.

_____

_____

Collins *Spotlight on Poetry* Activity Masters
© HarperCollins*Publishers* 1999

Cinquain Prayer, February Night, 1349 Cinquain, 1415 Cinquain

Use these notes on two other important historical events to help you write cinquains.

When you write your cinquain:

- Add to it
- Shorten it
- Change it
- Rewrite until it is just right and follows the pattern of syllables exactly.

1666 Great Fire of London

Started in Pudding Lane when someone knocked over a candle in a baker's shop.

Spread quickly because houses were made of wood and the streets were very narrow.

People tore down houses in an attempt to make firebreaks.

They brought water from the River Thames.

But the fire still spread, and burnt for four days.

1916 Life in the trenches

Dug deep into the mud.

The trenches filled with water.

Everything was wet and muddy.

Soldiers waited to be ordered 'over the top' and into battle.

Sometimes they received letters from home.

They could hear the sound of gunfire in the distance.

Elegy For Grandad

Reread the first verse of the poem which gives a detailed description of Grandad.

Think of someone you know well. Write down words and phrases that describe…

| what they look like | their personality | how they behave |

What adjectives describe them exactly?

_____ _____ _____

_____ _____ _____

_____ _____ _____

_____ _____ _____

Use this list of words and phrases to help you write a detailed, vivid description of this person.

Collins *Spotlight on Poetry* Activity Masters
© HarperCollins*Publishers* 1999

Use a dictionary which includes **etymological** information to discover the origins of these words.

lunatic
umbrella
alphabet
galaxy
ugly
disaster
lens
circus
October
hippopotamus

Sea Lions

List three **synonyms** for these words from the poem.
Write definitions explaining exactly how they differ
in meaning.

nudge

synonym   definition

1._____   _____

2._____   _____

3._____   _____

swift

synonym _____definition

1._____   _____

2._____   _____

3._____   _____

fall

synonym _____definition

1._____   _____

2._____   _____

3._____   _____

twist

synonym _____definition

1._____   _____

2._____   _____

3._____   _____

Collins *Spotlight on Poetry* Activity Masters
© HarperCollins*Publishers* 1999

Sea Lions

satin sea lions

Sink down, slide
In soft circles

climb
Up slapping
Their flippers

In these lines the poet uses the sounds of words to make the description more vivid and powerful.

Write a poem of your own:
- Choose something that makes interesting noises, for example, another animal or a machine.
- Write down words that you could use to describe it.
- Think about the sounds of the words as well as their meanings.
- Use these words to help you write a poem about the thing you have chosen.
- Try writing in very short lines, as in *Sea Lions*.

What am I?

chin-sticker   lip-gripper

Write **hyphenated** words like those above
to describe…

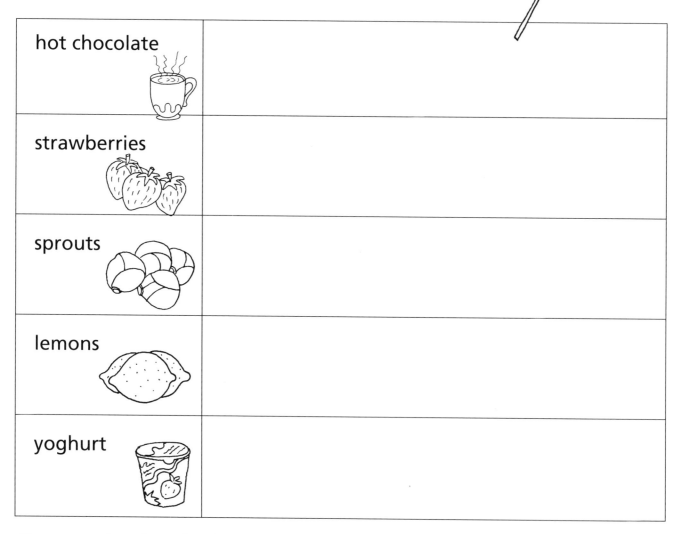

hot chocolate	
strawberries	
sprouts	
lemons	
yoghurt	

Choose a food or drink that you like or hate.

Write **hyphenated** words to describe it.

Reread the poem.

Underline or circle words and phrases that you find especially interesting or important in the poem.

Think about their meaning and their sound.

Write notes in the margins to explain why you think the poet chose these words.

Beyond the wildest waves

and below the raging sea

sunk deep in the dark green gloom

the guts of the Titanic

lie spilled on the ocean floor

lost in a battle of the swirls and swells

this mighty ship is stilled

its torn and twisted steel

wedged deep in the murky slime

as if crushed by a giant's fist

silent black shadows lurk

around ghostly open windows

a treasure trove of debris slips

into the shifting shape of the ocean sand

softly sighing in its watery grave

the massive hull stands proud and alone

rusticles dangling over portholes

like eyelashes with tears

the echoes of voices crying from the deep

are lost in the bubbling white surf

Collins *Spotlight on Poetry* Activity Masters
© HarperCollins*Publishers* 1999

Imagine you are one of the friends that the 'speaker' in the poem talks about.

Write a monologue that tells your side of the story.

You will need to:

● give the speaker in the poem a name
● describe events that lead up to the huff
● describe how you felt at the time
● describe how you feel now.

Look closely at the poem for clues.

Collins *Spotlight on Poetry* Activity Masters
© HarperCollins*Publishers* 1999

*A blowfly was **fuzzing***
At a window pane.
*The **tittering** clock*
Kept snatching the minutes away.

Write real or invented words to describe these sounds.

eating crisps 		
unwrapping a sweet 		
opening a can of fizzy drink 		
running through a puddle 		
kicking a football 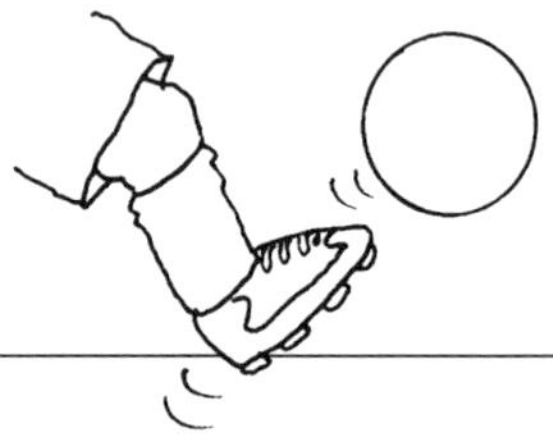		

Choose another noisy action. Write words to describe the sounds.

Collins *Spotlight on Poetry* Activity Masters
© HarperCollins*Publishers* 1999

If you think someone is acting in
a cowardly way, you might say:

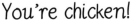

You're chicken!

Write down the animal idioms that are used when...

	when it is raining very hard
	when someone reveals a secret
	when someone is being very still and silent
	when something suspicious is going on
	when people are playing roughly
	when someone is being stubborn
	when someone takes the biggest part of something

Published by Collins Educational
An imprint of HarperCollins*Publishers*
77–85 Fulham Palace Road
Hammersmith
London W6 8JB

www.**fire**and**water**.com

© HarperCollins*Publishers* 1999

First published 1999

Reprinted 0 9 8 7 6 5 4 3 2 1

ISBN 0 00 310 356-0

Designed by Ken Vail Graphic Design
Cover Design by Clare Truscott

Printed and bound by Martins the Printers Ltd., Berwick-upon-Tweed

Collins Educational would like to thank the following teachers and
consultants who contributed to the research of this series:

Mrs J. Bibby (St Paul's C of E Primary School); Jason Darley, Liz Hooley (Jessop
Primary School); Mrs M.G. Farnell (High Meadow First School); Alison Lewis;
Chris Lutrario; Lesley Moores (Princess Royal Primary School); Sally Prendergrast
(Brooke Hill School); Jenny Ransom; Sheila Stamp (Castle Lower School);
Jill Walkinton; Sue Webb; Michael Webster (Castle Lower School);
Jill Wells (St Andrew's C of E Primary School).